Excerpts
of the F
Interna
the Litu
All right

Nihil Ob
Rev. Niall Sheehan
June, 2011

Revised 2017

Imprimatur:
Most Rev. J. McAreavey, D.D.
Bishop of Dromore
June, 2011

© Copyright
C.B.C. Distributors
Greenbank, Newry, Co. Down
Tel. 028 302 65216

Illustrations used with kind permission of:
Busquets - Spain

Printed in Italy

MY FIRST MISSAL

Edited by Rev. Niall Sheehan

Contains:
The New Order of the Mass
also Morning, Night and Occasional Prayers,
with specially selected prayers for
Confession and Communion.

WE STAND TOGETHER IN GOD'S HOUSE
Then the Priest says:

In the name of the Father,
and of the Son,
and of the Holy Spirit.
AMEN.

One of the following greetings is used:

1. The grace of our Lord Jesus Christ,
and the love of God,
and the communion of the Holy Spirit be with you all.
And with your spirit.

2. Grace to you and peace from God our Father
and the Lord Jesus Christ.
And with your spirit.

3. The Lord be with you.
And with your spirit.

We tell God we are sorry for our sins

WE SAY SORRY TO GOD

Brethren (brothers and sisters),
let us acknowledge our sins,
and so prepare ourselves to celebrate
the sacred mysteries.

I confess to almighty God
and to you, my brothers and sisters,
that I have greatly sinned,
in my thoughts and in my words,
in what I have done and in what I
have failed to do,
through my fault, through my fault,
through my most grievous fault;
therefore I ask blessed Mary
ever-Virgin,
all the Angels and Saints,
and you, my brothers and sisters,
to pray for me to the Lord our God.

We ask God
for his forgiveness

May almighty God have mercy on us,
forgive us our sins,
and bring us to everlasting life.
Amen.

....

You were sent to heal the
contrite of heart:
Lord, have mercy. or: Kyrie, eleison.
Lord, have mercy. or: Kyrie, eleison.
You came to call sinners:
Christ, have mercy. or: Christe, eleison.
Christ, have mercy. or: Christe, eleison.
You are seated at the right hand of
the Father to intercede for us:
Lord, have mercy. or: Kyrie, eleison.
Lord, have mercy. or: Kyrie, eleison.

May almighty God have mercy on us,
forgive us our sins,
and bring us to everlasting life.
Amen.

We praise you,
we bless you,
we adore you,
we glorify you,
we give you thanks.

THE GLORIA
We praise God

Glory to God in the highest,
and on earth peace to people
of good will.
We praise you,
we bless you,
we adore you,
we glorify you,
we give you thanks for your
  great glory,
Lord God, heavenly King,
O God, almighty Father.
Lord Jesus Christ,
Only Begotten Son,
Lord God, Lamb of God,
Son of the Father,
you take away the sins of the world,
  have mercy on us;
you take away the sins of the world,
  receive our prayer;
you are seated at the right hand of
  the Father,
  have mercy on us.

For you alone
are the Holy One,
you alone are
the Lord.

For you alone are the Holy One,
you alone are the Lord,
you alone are the Most High,
Jesus Christ,
with the Holy Spirit,
in the glory of God the Father.
Amen.

THE COLLECT PRAYER

Let us Pray.

We pray in silence to God our Father then the priest collects all our prayers in one prayer.

At the end of this prayer we all say:

Amen.

We listen to the word of God

GOD SPEAKS TO US. WE LISTEN.

READINGS
The word of the Lord.
Thanks be to God.

THE GOSPEL (*We all stand*)

The Lord be with you.
And with your spirit.

A reading from the holy Gospel according to ...
Glory to you, O Lord.

The Gospel of the Lord.
Praise to you, Lord Jesus Christ.

THE CREED
We profess our Faith

I believe in one God,
the Father almighty,
maker of heaven and earth,
of all things visible and invisible.

I believe in one Lord Jesus Christ,
the Only Begotten Son of God,
born of the Father before all ages.
God from God, Light from Light,
true God from true God,
begotten, not made,
consubstantial with the Father;
through him all things were made.
For us men and for our salvation
he came down from heaven,
and by the Holy Spirit was incarnate of the Virgin Mary,
and became man.

For our sake he was crucified
  under Pontius Pilate,
he suffered death and
  was buried,
and rose again on the third day
in accordance with the
  Scriptures.
He ascended into heaven
and is seated at the right hand
  of the Father.
He will come again in glory
to judge the living and the dead
and his kingdom will have no end.

I believe in the Holy Spirit,
the Lord, the giver of life,
who proceeds from the Father
  and the Son,
who with the Father and the Son
  is adored and glorified,
who has spoken through the
  prophets.

I believe in one, holy, catholic and apostolic Church.
I confess one Baptism for the forgiveness of sins
and I look forward to the resurrection of the dead
and the life of the world to come.
Amen.

Lord hear us

Lord graciously hear us

We present our gifts to God

THE PRESENTATION OF THE GIFTS OF BREAD AND WINE

Blessed are you, Lord God of all creation,
for through your goodness we have received
the bread we offer you:
fruit of the earth and work of human hands,
it will become for us the bread of life.

Blessed be God for ever.

Priest prays this quietly:
By the mystery of this water and wine
may we come to share in the divinity of Christ
who humbled himself to share in our humanity.

Blessed are you, Lord God of all creation,

for through your goodness we
   have received
the wine we offer you:
fruit of the vine and work of
   human hands,
it will become our spiritual drink.

Blessed be God for ever.

Pray, brethren (brothers and
   sisters),
that my sacrifice and yours
may be acceptable to God,
the almighty Father.

We give thanks to the Lord our God

May the Lord accept the
  sacrifice at your hands
for the praise and glory of
  his name,
for our good
and the good of all his
  holy Church.

PRAYER OVER THE OFFERINGS

Again the priest collects our prayers and offers them with our gifts to God our Father, to which we answer Amen.

THE EUCHARISTIC PRAYER
WE GIVE PRAISE AND THANKS TO GOD.

The Lord be with you.
And with your spirit.

Lift up your hearts.
We lift them up to the Lord.

Let us give thanks to the
  Lord our God.

It is right and just.

Preface
(From Eucharistic Prayer II)

It is truly right and just,
our duty and our salvation,
always and everywhere to give you
  thanks, Father most holy,
through your beloved Son,
  Jesus Christ,
your Word through whom you
  made all things,
whom you sent as our Saviour and
  Redeemer,
incarnate by the Holy Spirit
and born of the Virgin.

Fulfilling your will and gaining for
  you a holy people,
he stretched out his hands as he
  endured his Passion,
so as to break the bonds of death
and manifest the resurrection.

And so, with the Angels and all the Saints
we declare your glory,
as with one voice we acclaim:

Holy, Holy, Holy Lord God of hosts.
Heaven and earth are full of your glory.
Hosanna in the highest.
Blessed is he who comes in the name of the Lord.
Hosanna in the highest.

You are indeed Holy, O Lord,
the fount of all holiness

Eucharistic Prayer II

You are indeed Holy, O Lord,
the fount of all holiness.

Make holy, therefore, these
 gifts, we pray,
by sending down your Spirit upon
 them like the dewfall,
so that they may become for us
the Body and Blood of our Lord
 Jesus Christ.

At the time he was betrayed
and entered willingly into his
 Passion,
he took bread and, giving thanks,
 broke it,
and gave it to his disciples, saying:

TAKE THIS, ALL OF YOU,
AND EAT OF IT,
FOR THIS IS MY BODY,
WHICH WILL BE GIVEN UP FOR YOU.

In a similar way, when supper was ended,

he took the chalice

and, once more giving thanks,

he gave it to his disciples, saying:

TAKE THIS, ALL OF YOU, AND DRINK FROM IT,

FOR THIS IS THE CHALICE OF MY BLOOD,

THE BLOOD OF THE NEW AND ETERNAL COVENANT,

WHICH WILL BE POURED OUT FOR YOU AND FOR MANY

FOR THE FORGIVENESS OF SINS.

DO THIS IN MEMORY OF ME.

When we eat this
Bread and drink this Cup,
we proclaim your Death,
O Lord, until
you come again.

The mystery of faith.

We proclaim your Death, O Lord,
and profess your Resurrection
until you come again.

or:

When we eat this Bread
and drink this Cup,
we proclaim your Death, O Lord,
until you come again.

or:

Save us, Saviour of the world,
for by your Cross and
  Resurrection
you have set us free.

or: (In Ireland only)

My Lord and my God.

Gathered into one by the Holy Spirit

Therefore, as we celebrate
the memorial of his Death and
Resurrection,
we offer you, Lord,
the Bread of life and the Chalice
of salvation,
giving thanks that you have held
us worthy
to be in your presence and
minister to you.

Humbly we pray
that, partaking in the Body and
Blood of Christ,
we may be gathered into one by
the Holy Spirit.

Remember, Lord, your Church,
spread throughout the world,
and bring her to the fullness
of charity,
together with N. our Pope and N.
our Bishop, and all the clergy.

Remember also our brothers and sisters
who have fallen asleep in the hope of the resurrection,
and all who have died in your mercy:
welcome them into the light of your face.
Have mercy on us all, we pray,
that with the Blessed Virgin Mary, Mother of God,
with blessed Joseph, her Spouse,
with the blessed Apostles,
and all the Saints who have pleased you throughout the ages,
we may merit to be coheirs to eternal life,

and may praise and glorify you
through your Son, Jesus Christ.

Through him, and with him,
  and in him,
O God, almighty Father,
in the unity of the Holy Spirit,
all glory and honour is yours,
for ever and ever.

Amen.

WITH JESUS WE PRAY TO GOD OUR FATHER

At the Saviour's command
and formed by divine teaching,
we dare to say:

Our Father, who art
  in heaven,
hallowed be thy name;
thy kingdom come,
thy will be done
on earth as it is in heaven.
Give us this day our daily
  bread,
and forgive us our trespasses,
as we forgive those who
  trespass against us;
and lead us not into
  temptation,
but deliver us from evil.

Deliver us, Lord, we pray,
from every evil,
graciously grant peace in our days,
that, by the help of your mercy,
we may be always free from sin
and safe from all distress,
as we await the blessed hope
and the coming of our Saviour,
Jesus Christ.

For the kingdom,
the power and the glory are yours
now and for ever.

Lord Jesus Christ,
who said to your Apostles:
Peace I leave you, my peace
  I give you,
look not on our sins,
but on the faith of your Church,
and graciously grant her peace
  and unity
in accordance with your will.

Who live and reign for ever
  and ever.
Amen.

The peace of the Lord
be with you always.
And with your spirit.

Let us offer each other
the sign of peace.

Then the Priest prays quietly:
May this mingling of the
  Body and Blood
of our Lord Jesus Christ
bring eternal life to us who
  receive it.

Lamb of God, you take away the
  sins of the world,
have mercy on us.

Dear Jesus give me the grace to receive you always

Lamb of God, you take away the
  sins of the world,
have mercy on us.
Lamb of God, you take away the
  sins of the world,
grant us peace.

Behold the Lamb of God,
behold him who takes away
  the sins of the world.
Blessed are those called
  to the supper of the Lamb.

Lord, I am not worthy
that you should enter
  under my roof,
but only say the word
and my soul shall be healed.

*When giving Holy Communion,
the priest says:*
The Body of Christ.
Amen.

PRAYERS BEFORE COMMUNION

Lord Jesus, come to me.
Lord Jesus, give me your love.
Lord Jesus, come to me and give me yourself.

Lord Jesus, you are the bread of life.
Lord Jesus, feed me with the bread of life.
Lord Jesus, friend of children come to me.
Lord Jesus, you are my Lord and my God.
Praise to you, Lord Jesus Christ.

PRAYERS AFTER COMMUNION

Lord Jesus, I love and adore you.
You're a special friend to me.
Welcome, Lord Jesus,
oh welcome,
thank you for coming to me.

Thank you, Lord Jesus,
oh thank you,
for giving yourself to me.
Make me strong to show your love wherever I may be.

I'm ready now, Lord Jesus
to show how much I care.
I'm ready now to give your
love at home and everywhere.

Welcome, Lord Jesus,
welcome!
Lord Jesus, you are with me
now in all I say and do.
Welcome, Lord Jesus,
welcome!
All I say and do today
I say and do for you.

Be near me, Lord Jesus, I
ask you to stay,
close by me forever and love
me I pray.
Bless all of us children in
your loving care
and bring us to heaven to live
with you there.

PRAYER AFTER COMMUNION
The Priest thanks God our Father for all his gifts, especially his Son Jesus. At the end of this prayer we say: Amen

BLESSED AND SENT BY GOD
Given a mission to share and love

The Lord be with you.
And with your spirit.

May almighty God bless you,
the Father, and the Son,
and the Holy Spirit.

Amen.

1. Go forth, the Mass is ended.
2. Go and announce the Gospel of the Lord.
3. Go in peace, glorifying the Lord by your life.
4. Go in peace.

Thanks be to God.

We say our prayers

PRAYER TO MY GUARDIAN ANGEL

Angel of God, my guardian dear
to whom God's love
commits me here.
Ever this day be at my side
to light and guard,
to rule and guide.

Amen.

MORNING PRAYERS

Our Father, who art
in heaven,
hallowed be thy name;
thy kingdom come,
thy will be done
on earth as it is in heaven.
Give us this day our daily
bread,
and forgive us our trespasses,
as we forgive those who
trespass against us;
and lead us not into
temptation,
but deliver us from evil.

Hail Mary, full of grace, the Lord is with you, blessed are you among women and blessed is the fruit of your womb, Jesus. Holy Mary, Mother of God, pray for us sinners now, and at the hour of our death.
Amen.

Father in heaven, you love me, you're with me night and day. I want to love you always in all I do and say.
I'll try to please you, Father.
Bless me through the day.
Amen.

Glory be to the Father and to the Son and to the Holy Spirit as it was in the beginning is now and ever shall be world without end Amen.

Christ be with me
Christ be beside me
Christ be before me
Christ be behind me
Christ be at my right hand
Christ be at my left hand
Christ be with me
everywhere I go.
Christ be my friend,
for ever and ever.
Amen.

Holy Spirit, I want to do what is right.
Help me.
Holy Spirit, I want to live like Jesus.
Guide me.
Holy Spirit, I want to pray like Jesus.
Teach me.

We thank you, Lord, for this new day which is now beginning. Help us to spend it doing what we can for you and for others, especially those who need our help most.

NIGHT PRAYERS

God our Father, you love us and you care for us. You give us our family to look after us. You give us friends to play with us. You give us many people to love and help us. Bless and guide us everyday.

God bless everyone.

God, our Father, I come to say
thank you for your love today.

Thank you for my family
and all the friends you give to
me.

Guard me in the dark of night and
in the morning send your light.
Amen.

PRAYER TO OUR LADY

O Lord, through the help of the Blessed Virgin Mary heal the sick, comfort those who mourn, pardon sinners, give us all a share in your grace, and bring our deceased friends to the happiness of heaven.

PRAYER TO ST. JOSEPH

You, O God, created all things and gave work for men to do. May the example and prayers of St. Joseph help us to do our own work well and win us the reward you have promised.

PRAYER FOR PEACE

Lord, make me an instrument
of your peace.
Where there is hatred,
let me show love.
Where there is injury,
let me show pardon.
Where there is doubt,
let me show faith.
Where there is despair,
let me give hope.
Where there is darkness,
let me give light.
Where there is sadness,
let me give joy.

PRAYER FOR OUR FRIENDS

O God of all love, love our friends and teach them to love you with all their hearts, that they may think and speak and do only what is pleasing to you. We ask this through Christ Our Lord. Amen.

PRAYER TO A PATRON SAINT

God our Father you have given us Saint N. as our patron and friend. With their help may we learn to be kind and loving, wise and forgiving. Teach us to be generous and gentle to all we meet, so that all we say and do, think and pray may help us to choose the better way. Amen.

PRAYERS BEFORE CONFESSION

Lord Jesus, help me to make a good Confession,
Help me to remember the times I didn't love God and others.
Help me to be sorry,
Help me to make up my mind to be better.
Have mercy on me, oh Lord, and forgive me.
Mary my mother, pray for me.
O my God
I thank you for loving me.
I am sorry for all my sins,
for not loving others and not loving you. Help me to live like Jesus and not sin again.
Amen.

ACT OF SORROW

O my God,
I thank you for loving me.
I am sorry for all my sins.
For not loving others and not loving you.
Help me to live like Jesus and not sin again.

Amen.

PRAYERS AFTER CONFESSION

Lord Jesus, thank you for helping me to make a good Confession, and thank you for your love and forgiveness.
Help me, Lord Jesus, to love God the Father and others.

Mary, my mother, pray to Jesus for me.

Now say your Penance.

Prayer for Others

Lord Jesus bless my father, my mother, my brothers and sisters and all others I ought to pray for

Prayer for Help

Lord Jesus, help me to do what you want me to do. Help me to do my work better. Help me to be kind and thoughtful at home, and friendly to all my neighbours.

Our children without faith
will never be rich;
with faith, they will
never be poor.
Blessed Giuseppe Tovini